Praise for *When Helping Hurts Small Group Experience*

For over fifteen years I've worked alongside other Christians in efforts to effectively address poverty at home and abroad. I can honestly report that *When Helping Hurts* is the single best book I've seen on this topic. . . .

— **Amy L. Sherman, PhD**, *Senior Fellow and Director, Sagamore Institute Center on Faith in Communities; author of* Restorers of Hope

What an opportunity evangelicals have to make a difference in our world through the church as we move deeper into the third millennium! Corbett and Fikkert build on the growing momentum of holistic witness that's sweeping our country and globe. . . . *When Helping Hurts* will help the hurting—and us as well.

— **Dr. Ronald J. Sider,** *President, Evangelicals for Social Action; Professor of Theology, Holistic Ministry, and Public Policy, Palmer Theological Seminary; author of* Rich Christians in an Age of Hunger

Corbett and Fikkert fill some important gaps in our thinking and acting about poverty as Christians. Churches in North America will find this a helpful way to educate congregations and then motivate them to action, both globally and in their neighborhoods. . . .

— **Bryant L. Myers, PhD,** *Professor of International Development ,School of Intercultural Studies, Fuller Theological Seminary*

Steve and Brian have rung the bell—a clarion call to rethink how we apply the gospel to a broken world. *When Helping Hurts* lays out the principles and practice for transforming our good intentions into genuine, lasting change. I couldn't recommend this book more highly.

— **Stephan J. Bauman,** *Senior Vice President of Programs, World Relief*

Corbett and Fikkert have done a masterful job integrating insights from Scripture, social science research, and community development practice to give readers sound, practical, and effective strategies for equipping people to have more effective ministry to the poor. . . . *When Helping Hurts* should be required reading for all church leaders, academics, and church members.

   — **Dr. Steven L. Childers,** *President and CEO, Global Church Advancement; Associate Professor of Practical Theology, Reformed Theological Seminary-Orlando*

This is a book that every church leader should read. It takes the church beyond the common Band-Aid ministries to ministries that truly make a difference in the lives of the people they seek to serve. . . .

   — **Dr. L. Jean White,** *Coordinator for Church and Community Ministries, Ministry Evangelism Team, North American Mission Board*

When Helping Hurts is the most important book for the church to read as it seeks to serve the poor in ways that make a lasting difference. Corbett and Fikkert biblically define poverty, highlight why past initiatives haven't always lived up to expectations, and provide practical ways for extending the kingdom of God both in inner cities and to the ends of the earth.

   — **Peter Greer,** *President, HOPE International*

WHEN
HELPING
HURTS
. . .
THE SMALL GROUP
EXPERIENCE

STEVE CORBETT
and BRIAN FIKKERT

MOODY PUBLISHERS
CHICAGO

All Scripture quotations are taken from the Holy Bible, New International Version®, NIV®. Copyright © 1973, 1978, 1984 by Biblica, Inc.™ Used by permission of Zondervan. All rights reserved worldwide. www.zondervan.com. The "NIV" and "New International Version" are trademarks registered in the United States Patent and Trademark Office by Biblica, Inc.™

Crafted for the Chalmers Center by Katie Casselberry
Moody Publishers editor: Pam Pugh
Interior Design: Smartt Guys design
Cover Design: Faceout Studio, Emily Weigel
Cover Image: Veer/Image Source Photography/#SP2169787

ISBN: 978-0-8024-1156-3

All websites and phone numbers listed herein are accurate at the time of publication but may change in the future or cease to exist. The listing of website references and resources does not imply publisher endorsement of the site's entire contents. Groups and organizations are listed for informational purposes, and listing does not imply publisher endorsement of their activities.

We hope you enjoy this book from Moody Publishers. Our goal is to provide high-quality, thought-provoking books and products that connect truth to your real needs and challenges. For more information on other books and products written and produced from a biblical perspective, go to www.moodypublishers.com or write to:

Moody Publishers
820 N. LaSalle Boulevard
Chicago, IL 60610

3 5 7 9 10 8 6 4

Printed in the United States of America

CONTENTS

A NOTE TO LEADERS: HOW TO USE THIS SERIES

Over the past two decades, we have seen an enormous increase in the North American church's efforts to help the poor. We are incredibly excited about this development, but we are also concerned because we see this reenergized church doing many harmful things. Good intentions are not enough; it is possible to hurt poor people in the very process of trying to help them. The goal of this series is to equip the North American church with a ministry framework that restores the poor to fulfilling their God-given callings and potential.

We pray that God would use this series to affect your heart, your mind, and your actions, both as individuals and as a church community. Ultimately, that change is a work of the Holy Spirit. However, we do have a few suggestions about how to use this series.

Prepare for leading the group by reading *When Helping Hurts*; for your reference, we are listing the chapters of *When Helping Hurts* that correspond with each unit at the end of this opening section. Reading these chapters will give you a deeper personal understanding of the content, enabling you to facilitate class discussion more effectively.

We have designed each unit to be completed within an hour, though your discussion can certainly be extended beyond that. Each unit has the same basic components, as described below with rough time estimates:

OPEN (5–10 minutes): This section includes preliminary questions and an introductory paragraph. Discussing the preliminary questions as a group is a vital part of mentally and spiritually preparing for the rest of the unit. Use this time to foster an environment of openness and dialogue, creating a safe atmosphere where participants feel comfortable sharing their ideas, questions, and concerns.

WATCH (15–20 minutes): Encourage people to close their books while watching the video so that they can fully listen to and engage with the material.

APPLY (20 minutes): These questions are designed to create discussion—they do not have right or wrong answers. The goal is to foster reflection, understanding, and change in the participants' hearts. As such, it is important to give adequate time for discussion. Don't be afraid of a bit of silence, and don't be afraid of asking people to expand on their answers. You will find that having people wrestle with questions and issues together, so long as it is done in a spirit of respect, is enormously beneficial and even powerful.

CLOSE (5 minutes): Read this paragraph together as you conclude the session. Ask if anyone has questions. If there is not time to adequately discuss each one, ask the group to contemplate these questions throughout the week.

PRAY (5 minutes): Use this final statement and prayer prompt as a call for reflection and action. Encourage participants to return to this prompt as they pray throughout the week, and then close in prayer together.

GO DEEPER (flexible): If you have a longer Sunday school or small group session, consider using modules from the Go Deeper section once you have completed the basic discussion questions. You could also extend each unit over two weeks by completing the basic unit one week, followed by the Go Deeper materials the next week.

Please note that Go Deeper is made up of stand-alone modules with short text explanations and questions. You can pick and choose which additional modules you would like to use based on the makeup and interests of your group. If you do plan to use the Go Deeper section, it is particularly important that you have recently read *When Helping Hurts*. To that end, we have included page numbers from *When Helping Hurts* so that you can easily review the specific portions of the book covered in each module. Having extra background will be essential to explaining and facilitating discussion about the Go Deeper content. Further, we highly encourage you to have group members read the relevant sections of *When Helping Hurts*, particularly for those modules marked "Use in Conjunction with *When Helping Hurts*."

Go Deeper will enrich your study of these important topics. We encourage you to incorporate at least some of the modules as your group meets together.

In addition to these sections, we have included a series of Getting Started questions and a list of suggested resources. We are providing these materials so your group can begin taking concrete steps in more effectively responding to poverty in your immediate community. Working through the Getting Started portion will take considerable amounts of time and research. If your group is interested and committed to doing so, we recommend that you work on it together over the course of several weeks.

We cannot overemphasize the centrality of prayer in this series. The principles in this course require that each of us honestly examines our own heart and actions. Spend time praying that God would soften your heart and the hearts of the participants. But also pray that your group would see, internalize, and celebrate the hope rooted in the work of Christ. God is at work in this world, and we have the incredible joy and responsibility of joining in that work. Pray together at the beginning and end of each session, and encourage participants to pray with one another throughout the week.

Through the reconciling work of Christ, places as diverse as Atlanta, Georgia, and Kampala, Uganda, can be healed of their brokenness. Jesus Christ is making all things new, and it is the church's great privilege to proclaim that message. We are praying that this series can be a blessing as you live out that calling in your community.

—Steve Corbett and Brian Fikkert

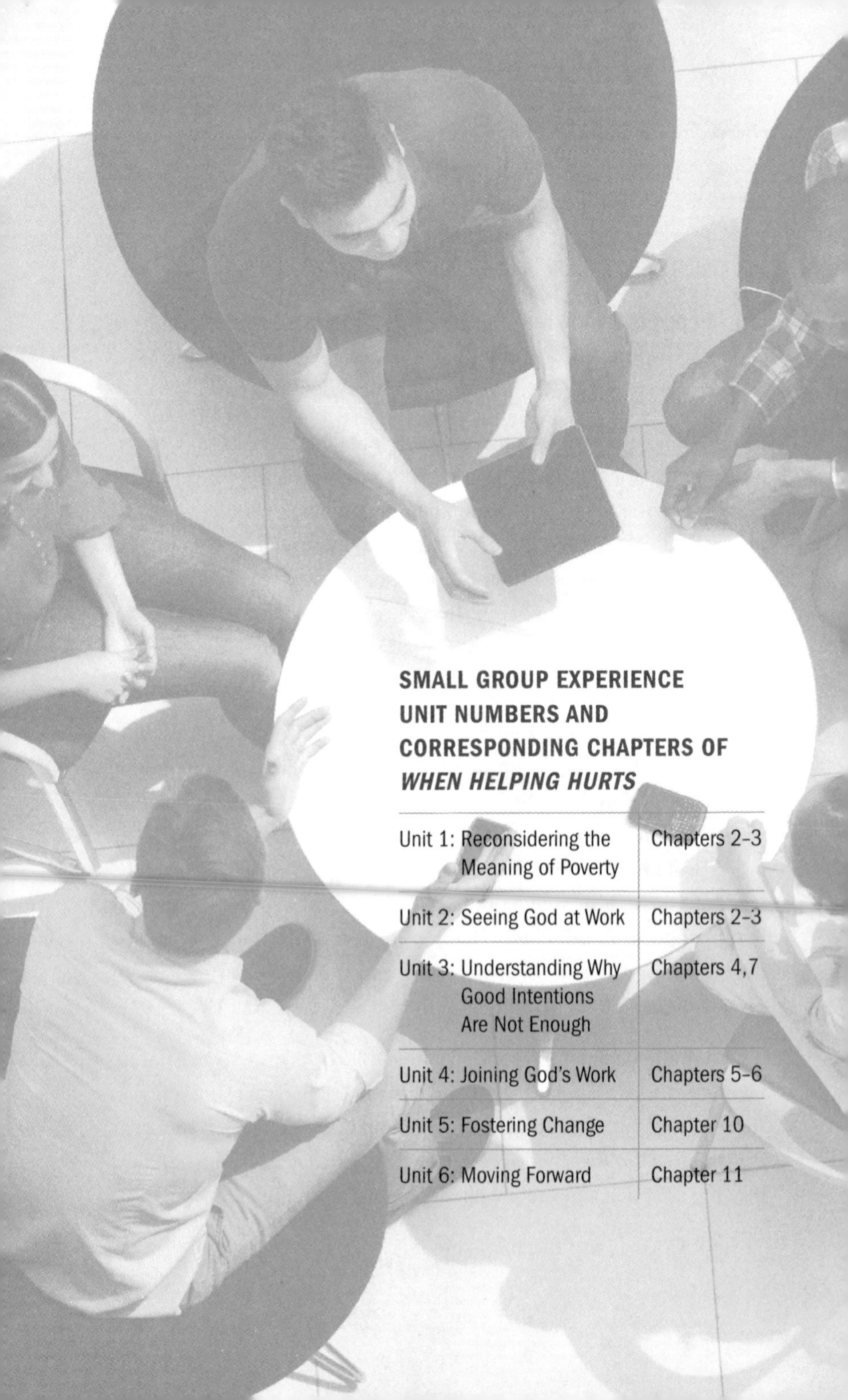

**SMALL GROUP EXPERIENCE
UNIT NUMBERS AND
CORRESPONDING CHAPTERS OF
*WHEN HELPING HURTS***

Unit 1: Reconsidering the Meaning of Poverty	Chapters 2-3
Unit 2: Seeing God at Work	Chapters 2-3
Unit 3: Understanding Why Good Intentions Are Not Enough	Chapters 4,7
Unit 4: Joining God's Work	Chapters 5-6
Unit 5: Fostering Change	Chapter 10
Unit 6: Moving Forward	Chapter 11

UNIT 1

RECONSIDERING THE MEANING OF **POVERTY**

OPEN

Discuss these questions before beginning this week's unit.

• What is poverty? List the first five to ten words or phrases that come to your mind when you think of poverty.

• List the first five areas (e.g., of your city, community, the world) that come to mind when you think of poverty.

What's the Problem?

The average North American enjoys a standard of living that has been unimaginable for most of human history. Meanwhile, 40 percent of the earth's inhabitants eke out an existence on less than two dollars per day. Indeed, the economic and social disparity between the haves and the have-nots is on the rise both within North America and between North America and much of the Majority World (Africa, Asia, and Latin America).

If you are a North American *Christian*, the reality of our society's vast wealth presents you with an enormous responsibility, for throughout the Scriptures God's people are commanded to show compassion to the poor. In fact, doing so is simply part of our job description as followers of Jesus Christ (Matthew 25:31–46). While the biblical call to care for the poor transcends time and place, passages such as 1 John 3:17 should weigh particularly heavily on the minds and hearts of North American Christians: "If anyone has material possessions and sees his brother in need but has no pity on him, how can the love of God be in him?"

WATCH

Close your books and use the accompanying QR code to watch this week's video.

www.helpingwithouthurting.org/smallgroup-1

APPLY

1. Did the words the materially poor used to describe poverty in the video differ from the words you listed in the preliminary questions? If so, what words and differences did you find most surprising?

2. The brokenness of the four relationships illustrated below can lead to behaviors and circumstances that contribute to poverty.

THE FOUR BROKEN RELATIONSHIPS

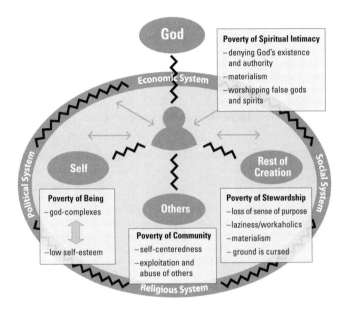

Adapted from Bryant L. Myers, *Walking with the Poor: Principles and Practices of Transformational Development* (Maryknoll, N.Y.: Orbis Books, 1999), 27.

Consider the story of a friend or family member who is poor. Where do you see evidence of each of the four broken relationships in his or her life? Can you see ways that this brokenness has led to his or her poverty?

• Broken Relationship with God:

• Broken Relationship with Self:

- Broken Relationship with Others:

- Broken Relationship with the Rest of Creation:

3. How might thinking about this person's poverty in terms of these broken relationships change the way you interact with him or her? Are there new ways you could show the love and healing work of Christ to this person or family in each of the broken relationships?

CLOSE *(or proceed to* **Go Deeper** *if time permits)*

Poverty is the result of broken relationships. But as we will explore in the rest of this series, broken relationships can be restored by the work of Christ. He came to make all things new, breaking the hold of sin and death "far as the curse is found." He came to show us that we can have a relationship with our Father, that we have dignity as creatures made in God's image, that we are to love one another in nourishing community, and that we have the privilege of stewarding the rest of creation. The fall has marred what God intended for us at creation, but the work of Christ offers hope that what is broken, both inside of us and around us, will be repaired. His victory over sin and death is certain, and His healing power is our comfort and peace. Let's walk together as we explore what God's reconciling work in this world looks like, and how we can effectively partner with Him in ministering to people who are poor.

PRAY

"Human beings are fundamentally wired to experience these four relationships. It's not all arbitrary, it's not all up for grabs. When we experience these relationships in the way that God intended them, we experience humanness in the way God intended."

Spend time this week praying that God would open your eyes to the beauty and potential around you, including in the lives of people who are poor. Pray that He would help you to break free of a material understanding of poverty, leading you to love and serve these people in ways that point them back to His original design for their lives.

GO DEEPER

Use one or more of the following modules to further explore principles of poverty alleviation.

THE ROOT OF POVERTY
(Reference *When Helping Hurts*, 52–54.)

"At that moment, it doesn't matter how much the doctor loves you. It doesn't matter how compassionate the doctor is, it doesn't matter how many good intentions the doctor has. . . . If the doctor misdiagnoses what's wrong with you, you won't get better, and you might get worse."

Look over the frequently cited causes of and responses to poverty below:

If We Believe the Primary Cause of Poverty Is . . .	Then We Will Primarily Try to . . .
A Lack of Knowledge	Educate the Poor

15

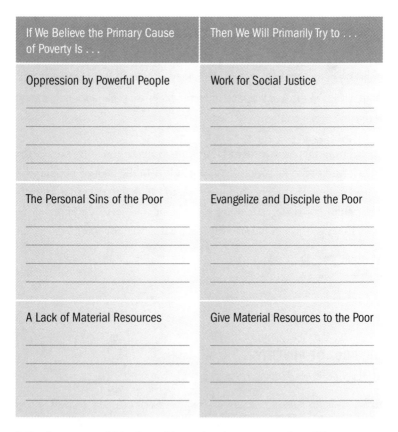

If We Believe the Primary Cause of Poverty Is . . .	Then We Will Primarily Try to . . .
Oppression by Powerful People	Work for Social Justice
The Personal Sins of the Poor	Evangelize and Disciple the Poor
A Lack of Material Resources	Give Material Resources to the Poor

1. In the space within the table, write down examples of how you or your church have built ministries to address the various causes of poverty. (For example, under "A Lack of Knowledge," you might write, "Students were dropping out of high school . . . so we started after-school tutoring programs.")

2. Does your work seem focused on addressing one particular cause?

3. How might each of the causes of poverty listed in the table actually flow from brokenness in the four relationships? How might this

deeper diagnosis impact the ways you interact with people around you who are poor?

BROKEN RELATIONSHIPS AND MATERIAL POVERTY[1]

(Reference *When Helping Hurts,* 54–59.)

When the four relationships are functioning properly, humans experience the fullness of life that God intended—we are being what God created us to be.

THE FOUR FOUNDATIONAL RELATIONSHIPS

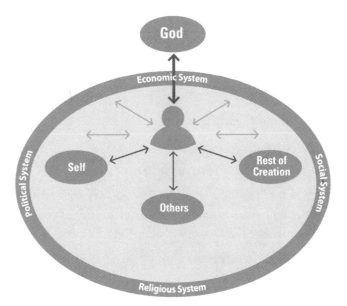

Adapted from Bryant L. Myers, *Walking with the Poor: Principles and Practices of Transformational Development* (Maryknoll, N.Y.: Orbis Books, 1999), 27.

But as we discussed in the video, the fall broke these relationships.

THE FOUR BROKEN RELATIONSHIPS

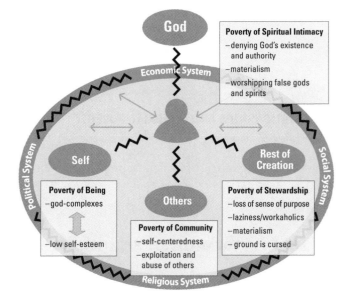

Adapted from Bryant L. Myers, *Walking with the Poor: Principles and Practices of Transformational Development* (Maryknoll, N.Y.: Orbis Books, 1999), 27.

From this framework, poverty isn't about a lack of material things. Instead, it is about much deeper issues:

POVERTY

"Poverty is the result of relationships that do not work, that are not just, that are not for life, that are not harmonious or enjoyable. Poverty is the absence of shalom in all its meanings."

—Bryant Myers, *Walking with the Poor*[2]

With this definition of poverty and the four broken relationships in mind, read the following story about Mary:

Mary lives in a slum in western Kenya. As a female in a male-dominated society, Mary has been subjected to polygamy, to regular physical and verbal abuse from her husband, and to fewer years of schooling than males. As a result, Mary lacks the confidence to look for a job.

Desperate, Mary decides to be self-employed, but needs a loan to get her business started. Unfortunately, the local loan shark exploits Mary, demanding an interest rate of 300 percent on her loan of twenty-five dollars. Having no other options, Mary borrows from the loan shark and, along with hundreds of others just like her, starts a business of selling homemade charcoal in the local market. The market is glutted with charcoal sellers, which keeps the prices very low. But it never even occurs to Mary to sell something else, because charcoal is the only resource she knows how to access. Frustrated by her entire situation, Mary goes to the traditional healer (shaman) for help. The healer tells Mary that her difficult life is a result of angry ancestral spirits that need to be appeased through buying and sacrificing a bull.

1. Where do you see each of the four broken relationships in Mary's story, and how does each specifically contribute to her material poverty?

• Broken Relationship with God:

• Broken Relationship with Self:

• Broken Relationship with Others:

• Broken Relationship with the Rest of Creation:

WORLDVIEW MATTERS[3]

(Use in conjunction with *When Helping Hurts*, 87–90.)

If we are to move forward in helping without hurting, we have to fully embrace a relational view of poverty, setting aside our tendency to view poverty as primarily a material condition that can be solved primarily with material things.

We are deeply conditioned by our society's modern worldview to view everything around us in material terms. Thus, the way that we act toward the materially poor often paints a faulty picture of the nature of God, self, others, and the rest of creation.

THE MODERN WORLDVIEW

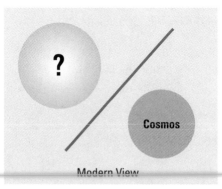

Adapted from Darrow L. Miller with Stan Guthrie, *Discipling the Nations: The Power of Truth to Transform Cultures* (Seattle, WA: YWAM, 2001), figures 1.7–1.10, pp. 43–4.

The modern worldview, sometimes called "Western secularism," holds that the spiritual realm does not even exist. The universe is fundamentally a machine with origins and operations rooted in natural processes that humans can master through their own reason.

The material definition of poverty emanates from the modern worldview's belief that all problems—including poverty—are fundamentally material in nature and can be solved by using human reason (science and technology) to manipulate the material world in order to solve those problems or achieve these goals.

BIBLICAL THEISM

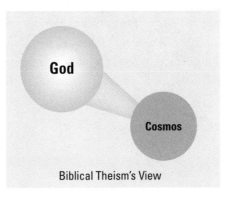

Biblical Theism's View

Adapted from Darrow L. Miller with Stan Guthrie, *Discipling the Nations: The Power of Truth to Transform Cultures* (Seattle, WA: YWAM, 2001), figures 1.7–1.10, pp. 43–4.

The worldview of biblical theism describes a God who is distinct from His creation but connected to it, a reality in which the spiritual and material realms touch each other. Indeed, Colossians 1 describes God, in the person of Jesus Christ, as the Creator, Sustainer, and Reconciler of all things, including the material world. Thus, our approach to poverty alleviation should reflect this worldview, addressing the materially poor's physical and spiritual needs, not just one or the other.

1. When you get sick, what do you do?

2. Read 2 Chronicles 16:7–9 and Psalm 20:6–8. What was Asa's sin?

3. Because of the ways we have unintentionally accepted the modern worldview, we tend to rely on science and our own reason to solve our problems. We forget to call on the one who created and upholds the universe. Are you like Asa? How does your worldview need to be transformed to reflect a biblical understanding of God and creation?

UNIT 2

SEEING GOD AT **WORK**

OPEN

Discuss these questions as you read this week's introduction.

• If Alisa showed up at your church door next Sunday asking for help, what would you do?

• How would you define success in your efforts to help Alisa? What would her new "story" look like?

Are We There Yet?

During the 1990s, Alisa Collins and her family lived in one of America's most dangerous public housing projects in inner-city Chicago.[1] Alisa got pregnant at the age of sixteen, dropped out of high school, and started collecting welfare checks. She has five children from three different fathers, none of whom help with childrearing. With few skills, no husband, and limited social networks, Alisa struggled to raise her family in an environment characterized by widespread substance abuse, failing schools, high rates of unemployment, rampant violence, teenage pregnancy, and an absence of role models.

From time to time, Alisa tried to get a job, but a number of obstacles prevented her from finding and keeping regular work. First, there were simply not a lot of decent-paying jobs for high school dropouts living in ghettos. Second, the welfare system penalized Alisa for earning money, taking away benefits for every dollar she earned and for every asset she acquired. Third, Alisa had child-care issues that made it difficult to keep a job. Finally, Alisa felt inferior and inadequate. When she tried to get vocational training or a job and faced some obstacle, she quickly lost confidence and rapidly retreated back to where she was comfortable—public housing and welfare checks. Alisa felt trapped, and she and her family often talked about how they couldn't get out of the ghetto.

WATCH

Close your books and use the accompanying QR code to watch this week's video.

www.helpingwithouthurting.org/smallgroup-2

APPLY

1. You may not be materially poor, but what evidence do you see in your own life of the four broken foundational relationships? In what areas do you need to repent and pray for God's healing?

THE FOUR BROKEN RELATIONSHIPS

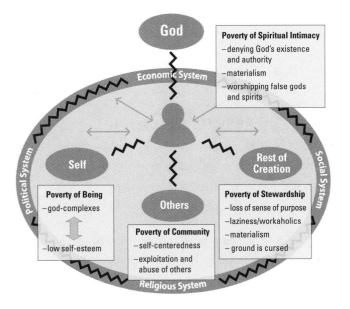

Adapted from Bryant L. Myers, *Walking with the Poor: Principles and Practices of Transformational Development* (Maryknoll, N.Y.: Orbis Books, 1999), 27.

• Broken Relationship with God:

• Broken Relationship with Self:

• Broken Relationship with Others:

• Broken Relationship with the Rest of Creation:

2. Read through the definition of poverty alleviation below:

POVERTY ALLEVIATION

A process in which people, both the materially poor and non-poor, move closer to living in right relationship with God, self, others, and the rest of creation.

• Think back to a situation in which you tried to minister to people who were materially poor. Did your approach reconcile the four broken relationships in each of you? In what ways?

• Were there any ways that your approach actually contributed to greater "poverty" in the four relationships in each of you? If so, what could you do differently in the future?

3. Look back at Alisa's story at the beginning of this unit. Given what we have talked about so far, including the quote below, what do you think "success" would look like in her story?

"If you go back to what is poverty, poverty alleviation isn't just about fixing their circumstances. It is about helping them discover that they are an image bearer and that they have tremendous value as a human being, that they are called to be a steward of their resources and opportunities."

• In what specific ways would her life be different?

• What personal choices would Alisa need to make, with God's help, to move out of poverty?

• What changes in systemic factors or circumstances—challenges Alisa has no control over—would aid Alisa in the process of moving out of poverty?

• With this new "story" in mind, how could you or your church help people like Alisa when they walk into your church?

CLOSE *(or proceed to* **Go Deeper** *if time permits)*

After decades of living on welfare checks, Alisa Collins started finishing her high school degree, working full-time as a kindergarten teacher, and getting up at 4:00 a.m. to wash her family's clothes before she was due at work. What happened?

It all began when Miss Miller, the principal of the local school, hired Alisa to work part-time as a teacher's aide. Miss Miller soon observed that Alisa had natural teaching gifts and took the time to encourage Alisa to pursue a teaching career, guiding her to the education and certification she would need. With Miss Miller's relational and nurturing approach, Alisa began to gain confidence. And while her view of herself was changing, two important changes also occurred in Alisa's economic environment. First, Congress passed welfare-reform legislation, making welfare more "pro-work" and placing limits on the length of time people could stay on it. Alisa knew her days on welfare were coming to an end and that she simply had to find a full-time job. Second, Miss Miller offered Alisa a job as a full-time teacher.

Churches are uniquely positioned to provide the relational ministry on an individual level that people like Alisa need. Of course, churches can also offer Alisa something that Miss Miller could not: a clear articulation of the gospel so that Alisa can experience the profound and lasting change of material poverty alleviation—*the ability to fulfill her calling of glorifying God through her work and life.*

PRAY

"Jesus Christ transforms both of us . . . Poverty alleviation is about walking side by side, hand in hand, and saying 'I'm broken, you're broken' but Jesus Christ can show up and bring healing to both of us."

Spend time this week praying that God would reveal your need for His miraculous reconciling work in your own heart, and that He would show you ways you can be a channel of that work to others in your community.

GO DEEPER

Use one or more of the following modules to further explore principles of poverty alleviation.

WORK, WORSHIP, AND POVERTY ALLEVIATION

(Reference *When Helping Hurts*, 73–75.)

"It is very hard to beg. You know, if I come to you to ask for things, I've got to come down." —Sarah Kasule

While we are all poor in the sense that we are all experiencing less than the fullness that God intended for us at creation, the materially poor face a daily struggle to survive that creates feelings of helplessness, anxiety, suffocation, shame, and desperation that are simply unparalleled in most of our lives. Thus, the definition of material poverty alleviation has its own unique dynamics:

> ## MATERIAL POVERTY ALLEVIATION
> Working to reconcile the four foundational relationships so that people can fulfill their callings of glorifying God by working and supporting themselves and their families with the fruit of that work.

Note these two things about the definition of material poverty alleviation:

- Material poverty alleviation involves more than ensuring that people have sufficient material things. Rather, it involves the much harder task of empowering people to *earn* sufficient material things through their own labor, for in doing so people are moved closer to being what God created them to be.

- Work is an act of worship. When people fulfill their callings by glorifying God in their work, praise Him for their gifts and abilities, and see both their effort and its products as an offering to Him, then work is an act of worship to God.

1. Think about your past and present work: Do you *believe* and *act* like the purpose of work is to glorify God?

2. What gifts has God given you? List gifts that are both specific (skills and talents) and more general (personality strengths, things you have learned from past experience, etc.).

3. In what ways has your work, present or past, utilized these gifts?

4. Think about your materially poor friends or family members. What gifts do you see in them that they could use to God's glory and to support themselves through work?

CHRIST IS MAKING ALL THINGS NEW

(Reference *When Helping Hurts*, 76–79.)

"The church is Grand Central Station for the Kingdom of God. The church is the primary manifestation of the Kingdom of God, and Christ is the one who alleviates poverty."

As the local church, we are to display God's reconciling work to the materially poor. Jesus is not just "beaming up" our souls out of planet Earth in Star Trek fashion because things are broken and messy; rather, Jesus is bringing reconciliation to every last speck of the universe, including both our foundational relationships and the systems that emanate from them. *Poverty is rooted in broken relationships, so the solution to poverty is rooted in the power of Jesus' death and resurrection to put all things into right relationship again.*

1. Read the following passages of Scripture. What do these passages say (explicitly or implicitly) about what God is doing and will ultimately accomplish in this world? How are you and your church demonstrating this work to the materially poor?

   • Colossians 1:15–20:

   • 2 Corinthians 5:17–20:

   • Revelation 21:1–4:

2. Can materially poor people participate fully in your church's corporate worship and fellowship? What obstacles might they encounter to being full participants? What might you do to address these obstacles?

As we walk with the materially poor over time in relationships, we also have to remember that Christ has been active in these communities since the creation of the world. This should give us a sense of humility and awe as we enter poor communities, for part of what we see there reflects the very hand of God. Of course, the residents of these communities may not recognize that God has been at work. In fact, they might not even know who God is. So part of our task may include introducing the community to who God is, proclaiming the good news of Christ's reconciling work through the cross and the empty tomb.

3. Think about a time in the past when you or your church ministered to the materially poor. Did your efforts include both a clear, verbal articulation of the gospel *and* a concrete demonstration of Christ's concern for restoring their four relationships—and thus His concern for healing their material poverty?

HELPING OR HURTING?

(Reference *When Helping Hurts*, 61–64.)

"We've just been steeped in this society that values and judges people based on what they have and what they have accomplished, so we are always going to be fighting falling back into this default mode of 'They need me, they need what I know, they need what I have.'" —*Jerilyn Sanders*

One of the biggest problems in many poverty-alleviation efforts is that they exacerbate the poverty of being of the economically rich—their god-complexes—and the poverty of being of the economically poor—their feelings of inferiority and shame.

When combined with our material understanding of poverty, the results can be devastating. We may help improve people's physical conditions—they may have clean water, repaired houses, or new classrooms—but the other, intangible aspects of their poverty are deepened. The equation below summarizes this dynamic:

Material Definition of Poverty	+	God-complexes of Materially Non-Poor	+	Feelings of Inferiority of Materially Poor	=	Harm to Both Materially Poor and Non-Poor

- Does this equation describe the work of you, your church, or other ministries in your community? If so, what steps can you take to move toward a healthier ministry dynamic?

ESCAPING THE POVERTY TRAP
(Reference *When Helping Hurts*, 84–87.)

"When you have a poverty of spirit, your hope diminishes, your sense of confidence erodes, and you begin to believe that for you there is no way out. It is what I would call conditioned hopelessness." —Robert Lupton

Whether we realize it or not, the fall had an impact on *everything* in our lives and the lives of the materially poor in deeply debilitating ways.

1. Have you ever felt trapped by life's circumstances to the point where you believed that you could not do anything to change the situation? If so, describe the emotions and behaviors that this produced in you. Did you ever feel like just giving up?

2. Do you see this sense of entrapment at work in the lives of the materially poor around you? If so, in what ways might you practically model and encourage them with the hope of Christ's reconciliation and restoration?

Consider Alisa's story. While Alisa's worldview, values, and behaviors clearly contributed to her material poverty, as an African-American woman growing up in a ghetto, she is also a victim of powerful systemic forces that have dealt her a different set of cards than those most North Americans received. The ghetto into which Alisa was born, through no choice of her own, was shaped by centuries of racial discrimination and damaging economic, social, and political factors. What happens when society crams historically oppressed, uneducated, unemployed, and relatively young human beings into high-rise buildings, provides them with inferior education, healthcare, and employment systems, and then establishes financial disincentives for work? Is it really that surprising that we see out-of-wedlock pregnancies, broken families, violent crimes, and drug trafficking?

Being aware of this background makes all the difference when Alisa walks into our church asking for assistance. Does Alisa have personal sins and behaviors that are contributing to her material poverty? Yes. But to reduce her problem to this ignores the comprehensive impact of the fall on both individuals and systems, blinding us to our need to bring the reality of Christ's redemption to bear on both.

3. When you interact with the materially poor, do you tend to see their poverty more as a result of their individual choices or their circumstances?

4. If you emphasize one more than the other, how would the way you interact with the materially poor change if you truly believed that the fall impacts both individual hearts and social systems?

UNIT 3

UNDERSTANDING WHY GOOD INTENTIONS ARE NOT **ENOUGH**

OPEN

Discuss these questions before beginning this week's unit.

• Think about the materially poor people in North America who have asked you or your church for immediate financial assistance. Under what conditions would you give things or money to these people? Be specific.

• Think about any ministry to the materially poor that you or your church has conducted in the Majority World, for example, a short-term mission trip. Under what conditions would you or your church give things or money to these people? Be specific.

• Are your answers to the previous two questions the same or different? Why or why not?

Not All Poverty Is Created Equal

You turn on the evening news and see that a tsunami has devastated Indonesia, leaving millions without food, adequate clothing, or shelter. Following a commercial break, the news returns and features a story about a low-income community in your city where many people are also without adequate food, clothing, or shelter. At first glance, the appropriate responses to each of these crises might seem to be very similar. The people in both situations need food, clothing, and housing, and providing these things to both groups seems to be the obvious solution.

But there is something nagging at the back of our minds as we reflect on these stories. Without a doubt, we are called to do something. But what? Deep down, do these people require different types of help? Recognizing that poverty is about more than just a lack of material resources, how can we engage in effective poverty alleviation in each of these contexts?

WATCH

Close your books and use the accompanying QR code to watch this week's video.

www.helpingwithouthurting.org/smallgroup-3

APPLY

1. Reflect on your answers to the preliminary questions at the start of this unit. Have your views changed at all? If so, how?

2. Describe a time when you ministered to a materially poor person or community. Now look at the diagram and definitions below. Were you providing relief, rehabilitation, or development?

RELIEF, REHABILITATION, AND DEVELOPMENT

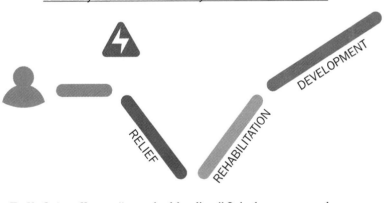

- **Relief**: An effort to "stop the bleeding." It is the urgent and temporary provision of emergency aid to reduce immediate suffering from a natural or man-made crisis, and it primarily utilizes a provider-receiver dynamic.

- **Rehabilitation**: An effort to restore people back to their pre-crisis state after the initial bleeding has stopped. In rehabilitation, people begin to contribute to improving their situation.

- **Development**: Walking with people across time in ways that move all the people involved—both the "helpers" and the "helped"—

closer to being in right relationship with God, self, others, and the rest of creation than they were before. It avoids "doing for" and focuses on "doing with."

3. Now think about the materially poor person or community you were ministering to: Do you think their circumstances required relief, rehabilitation, or development? Did you provide the appropriate intervention? If not, how could you change your approach to make it more effective in the future?

CLOSE *(or proceed to* **Go Deeper** *if time permits)*

By this point, you are probably realizing that poverty alleviation is far more complex than you initially thought. Residents of low-income communities in the United States and tsunami victims in Indonesia are experiencing poverty in unique ways, and thus require unique responses. If we do not recognize these nuances, we really can do harm in the midst of our well-intentioned efforts to help. But do not be discouraged. *It is God's work, not ours.* God is the one at work. God is the one restoring all things. *The joy of serving in God's kingdom is that He does not require perfection from us; rather, He asks us to be faithful servants who learn from our mistakes.* The success or failure of His cosmic plan is not contingent on whether or not we "perfectly" engage in poverty alleviation. In fact, we never will do it perfectly. Do not let the realization of any past mistakes you have made lead you to paralysis or fear.

No, good intentions aren't enough. We need to be wise in how we alleviate poverty. But if we stop ministering to the materially poor out of our fear of "doing it wrong," we are letting our god-complexes get in the way. We are acting as though our efforts are the bottom line, rather than the God who can use our humble—albeit imperfect—service for His glory and kingdom. The next units will focus on steps we can take to move forward in helping without hurting the materially poor or ourselves, trusting God to use us as agents of His reconciling work.

PRAY

"Give money to people to start businesses, you come a month later, and there is nothing. What you did was just increase their consumption. Then you realize that there was [a deeper] problem [in] their hearts, rather than in their hands. So transformation starts in the head, but it also sinks deeply into the heart, and hopefully that heart is transformed into their hands. So that is what we work towards." —Alvin Mbola

This week, spend time in prayer asking God to grant you a spirit of humility, joy, and perseverance as you consider how you can better walk with the materially poor. Pray that God would keep you dependent on His power as you seek transformation in your head, heart, and hands—and those of the materially poor.

GO DEEPER

Use one or more of the following modules to further explore principles of poverty alleviation.

THE POISON OF PATERNALISM
(Reference *When Helping Hurts*, 109–13.)

"When you give free things . . . they will not own that money, they will misuse that money . . . When you give them free things, it is like you are lowering their dignity and increasing the poverty level." —*Rachel Sang*

When we apply relief, rehabilitation, and development inappropriately, we do more than just "give people the wrong things." We are setting up a disempowering dynamic of paternalism.

PATERNALISM:
Habitually doing things for people that they can do for themselves.[1]

Paternalism can take a number of forms, such as:

- **Resource Paternalism:** giving people resources they do not truly need and/or could acquire on their own

- **Spiritual Paternalism:** taking spiritual leadership away from the materially poor, assuming we have more to offer than they do

- **Knowledge Paternalism:** assuming we have all the best ideas about how to do things

- **Labor Paternalism:** doing work for the materially poor that they could do for themselves

- **Managerial Paternalism:** taking ownership of change away from the poor, insisting that they follow our "better, more efficient" way of doing things

1. In what specific ways do you think paternalism could damage our own four foundational relationships (relationship with God, self, others, and the rest of creation) and those of the materially poor?

2. Look back at the example you discussed in Apply questions two and three. Was there any paternalism evident in your work? If so, in what way?

A DIFFERENT SORT OF ALLEVIATION

(Use in conjunction with *When Helping Hurts*, 99–109.)

"The key dynamic in development work is promoting an empowering process. . . . Development is as much about how you do the work as about what the work itself is."

Beyond simply providing different forms of assistance, the relational dynamics at play in relief, rehabilitation, and development are vastly different.

• **Relief**: The primary relational dynamic is a provider-receiver dynamic—assistance is "given to" or "done for" the materially poor.

• **Rehabilitation**: The relational dynamic transitions from directly "doing for" the materially poor to "doing with" the materially poor in a shared process and endeavor.

• **Development**: The primary dynamic is "walking with" the materially poor over time, rather than "doing for" them.

Now take a minute to review the definition of material poverty alleviation below:

MATERIAL POVERTY ALLEVIATION

Working to reconcile the four foundational relationships so that people can fulfill their callings of glorifying God by working and supporting themselves and their families with the fruit of that work.

1. Considering the different relational dynamics in relief and development, how might providing relief when development is the needed intervention contradict or undermine the process of material poverty alleviation?

2. Can you think of any examples where you have seen this happen?

Remember: God, who is a worker, ordained work so humans could worship Him through their work. Engaging in paternalism or applying relief inappropriately causes the beneficiaries to abstain from work. This exacerbates their sense of powerlessness, and discourages them from glorifying God by using their God-given gifts to support themselves and their families.[2]

MINISTRY ASSESSMENT

(Reference *When Helping Hurts*, 99–115.)

(If you choose to complete this module, please first complete "The Poison of Paternalism" module above.)

Answer the questions below for your broader sphere of ministry. You already discussed parts of these questions in the Apply section, but you only referenced one specific example. This may take time, but it is a crucial step in moving toward helping without hurting in your community.

1. Make a list of the ministries that you and/or your church are involved in within your community *and* in the Majority World. Next to each ministry, write whether they are providing relief, rehabilitation, or development.

2. Now think about the materially poor individuals or communities each ministry is designed to reach. Do their circumstances require relief, rehabilitation, or development? Are your ministries providing the appropriate intervention? If not, what changes could you make to improve your approach?

3. For the ministries you mentioned above, discuss whether any forms of paternalism make an appearance in your work. If so, in what ways could you modify the ministry to make it more effective and appropriate?

SHORT-TERM MISSIONS AND PRINCIPLES OF POVERTY ALLEVIATION
(Use in conjunction with *When Helping Hurts*, 155–58; 161–63.)

Some of the principles of poverty alleviation, such as the danger of providing relief instead of development, strike an intuitive chord when working with the materially poor in North America. But many of us ignore these principles when working with the materially poor in the Majority World—particularly in the context of short-term missions. The poverty we see in the Majority World seems so extreme that we immediately gravitate toward giving things to people, regardless of whether or not they are capable of improving their own circumstances.

One of the reasons that this happens is that many short-term missions (STMs) to poor communities reflect the perspective of "poverty as deficit," the idea that poverty is due to the poor lacking something. North Americans often view the "something" as material resources, knowledge, or spirituality.[3] This conception of poverty leads to poverty-alleviation strategies in which the materially non-poor are necessarily in the position of giving the "something" to the materially poor, since the non-poor have the "something" and the poor do not have it. Further, because of the short duration of STMs, all of the "something" has to be given in the space of a week or two.

1. Look back at the definitions of relief, rehabilitation, and development. Which of the interventions do you think a STM team could or could not effectively provide? Why or why not?

2. If you have been involved in STMs before, were you working in contexts requiring relief, rehabilitation, or development? Did your team engage in or support the correct intervention?

3. Did your work exhibit any forms of paternalism? If so, how might you avoid this pitfall in the future?

DOING SHORT-TERM MISSIONS WITHOUT DOING LONG-TERM HARM
(Use in conjunction with *When Helping Hurts*, 163–67.)

Short-term missions (STMs) can be designed and practiced in ways that bless both team members and the receiving community. Discuss the following guidelines together, reflecting on how you might move toward an even better approach to STMs.

• Consider the real monetary cost of the STM and determine if it is the most responsible use of your resources. For example, $1,500 spent on a one-week trip would pay six to twelve months of salary for a committed local Christian community worker in many Majority World contexts. Seriously consider the pros and cons of other options, *and be willing to NOT go.*

• Design the trip to be more about learning from the local church and hosts, rather than doing particular projects or tasks.

• Only go where invited by local organizations that understand the relational nature of poverty and are focused on holistic development work.

• Contextualize the STM in the service of a local organization that is functioning effectively in appropriate relief, rehabilitation, and/or development roles.

• Keep teams small—you should be able to come and go as seamlessly as possible.

• Be sure team members are truly interested in learning about and supporting poverty alleviation, rather than seeking an adventure, vacation, or an emotional high.

• Make pre-trip learning and personal monetary contributions (not just from family or friends, but from one's own hard-earned cash) requirements of participation.

• Consider your work as part of a long-term process, not an individual project.

• Coordinators should be keenly aware of the tendency of the outsider to suffer from a god-complex and of the impoverished community to suffer a sense of inferiority.

• Be aware of inevitable cultural collisions that the team and host community will experience. Prepare for these encounters in the pre-trip learning.

Think about any STMs you have been a part of or STMs your church is in the process of planning:

1. Roughly how much per person did this trip cost? Can you think of any alternative things you could do with your missions or ministry budgets that might have greater impact than STMs? What are some specific actions you can take to investigate those alternatives?

2. Did the STM teams partner with already existing ministries and the local church?

• Did the team allow these local ministries to design and lead your work?

• What role did materially poor families and communities have in designing and accomplishing the work?

3. Think about the STM trips that your church is planning for the future. Referencing the list above, discuss three or four specific things you can do to improve these trips. How will you accomplish these changes in your church?

UNIT 4

JOINING GOD'S **WORK**

Discuss these questions before beginning this week's unit.

• Imagine that your church or ministry wants to help an individual poor person or a poor community. Who would you ask for advice? Write down a list of the people you might consult to design your approach.

• Was there ever a time when someone recognized a gift or ability in you that you did not even realize you possessed? How did that experience affect you?

More Than Meets the Eye

You have realized that unlike the Indonesian community devastated by the tsunami, the materially poor local community you saw on the nightly news requires development, not relief. But what do you do next? It seems like the next step would be to determine the needs of the individual or community, thus identifying the best way to help. In fact, many ministries do begin this way, using an interview or a survey to determine what is wrong and the best way to provide assistance. This needs-based approach has merit. After all, diagnosing the underlying problems is essential to forming the proper solutions, though other angles need to be considered as we begin the process of helping without hurting. *How* we engage in poverty alleviation is just as important as *what* we do.

WATCH

Close your books and use the accompanying QR code to watch this week's video.

www.helpingwithouthurting.org/smallgroup-4

APPLY

1. Look back at your answer to the first preliminary question in this unit. Who did you ask for advice? Who did you not ask for advice? What, if anything, does this reveal about your views of the materially poor and of yourself?

2. In light of the quote below, reflect on the materially poor people in your life. What God-given gifts do you see in them? Do you think that these people are aware of their gifts?

"One of the things that we have to come to believe is that everyone has something to contribute in the life of the community, that no one is so poor that they have nothing to bring to the exchange." —Robert Lupton

3. Consider the quote and definitions below:

"God has given everybody inherent dignity and worth and value, and when you set up a situation where you forget that, where you feel like you are just a little bit better than [the materially poor] . . . you are set up [for] failure. You get the nice, polite nods, but you don't get transformation." —Jerilyn Sanders

NEEDS-BASED DEVELOPMENT

A development approach that focuses on the deficits and shortcomings in the life of a person or community

ASSET-BASED DEVELOPMENT

A development approach that focuses on identifying, mobilizing, and connecting the God-given capabilities, skills, and resources of a person or community

• Take a moment to assess how you interact with the materially poor. Do you think that your actions, words, and attitude communicate to these people that they have valuable gifts and assets as image-bearers? In what ways?

- Are there any ways you can move toward an even more asset-based attitude and perspective?

CLOSE *(or proceed to* **Go Deeper** *if time permits)*

Our basic predisposition should be to see the poor communities around us—including their natural resources, people, families, neighborhood associations, schools, businesses, governments, culture, and so on—as being created by Jesus Christ and reflective of His goodness. Of course, the fall has distorted the inherent goodness of the creation design, damaging these assets. But all is not lost. As Colossians 1 shows us, Christ is holding all things together. He does not allow the effects of sin to completely destroy the inherent goodness of the assets that He created. In the midst of the decay, the assets persist—albeit in distorted fashion— because the Creator of the universe makes them persist. There is plenty of goodness to discover and to celebrate, even in a fallen world! But Christ is not just sustaining all things. He is also reconciling all things. One day all of the assets will be liberated from their "bondage to decay" (Romans 8:21). Jesus Christ created, sustains, and is redeeming assets in poor communities. As the body of Christ, the church should seek to do the same.

Asset-based, participatory development is not a recipe for automatic success in poverty alleviation. Nothing is. But because it begins by affirming the goodness of God's created order and the power of His redemptive work, it unleashes empowering dynamics that are crucial for fostering reconciliation—poverty alleviation—both in the materially poor and in ourselves.

PRAY

"Asking people to list their gifts and abilities is an empowering process . . . it is poverty alleviation."

Spend time in prayer this week asking God to open your eyes to the gifts He has placed in the lives of materially poor people around you, and to how you can encourage them to use those gifts to His glory.

GO DEEPER

Use one or more of the following modules to further explore principles of poverty alleviation.

"WHAT DO YOU THINK?"—PARTICIPATORY APPROACHES VS. BLUEPRINT APPROACHES

(Reference *When Helping Hurts*, 134–38.)

"Participation isn't just a means to getting the tractor used, it isn't just a means to making sure the well is taken care of. . . . Having people participate in stewarding their gifts and resources . . . is a valid end in its own right. It is what we are wired for. Participation is not just a means to an end, but a valid end in its own right."

One of the reasons so many poverty alleviation efforts are ineffective is because of inadequate participation of poor people in the process. A "blueprint approach," in which the economically non-poor make all the decisions about the project and then do the project *to* the economically poor, usually fails. The ultimate goal of the blueprint approach is often to develop a standardized product and then to roll out that product in cookie-cutter fashion on a massive scale. This is incredibly tempting due to our tendency to view poverty as primarily a *material* problem with *material* solutions.

But remember: The goal is to restore people to experiencing humanness in the way that God intended. The crucial thing is to help people to understand their identity as image-bearers, to love their neighbors as themselves, to be stewards over God's creation, and to bring glory to God in all things.

1. Have you experienced any contexts, whether in your office, your church, or your family, where you did or did not feel invited to participate in the group's actions or relationships? How did those experiences affect you?

2. Read the following verses and discuss how they might apply to developing asset-based, participatory ministries with the materially poor—particularly those who are believers:

• 1 Thessalonians 5:10–11:

• Philippians 4:8:

• 1 Corinthians 12:12–26:

• James 2:1–5:

THE ESSENTIALS OF ASSET-BASED, PARTICIPATORY DEVELOPMENT
(Reference *When Helping Hurts*, 119–22; 134–38.)

"Participation is core; it's often been said it's the engine of development. It's what creates ownership of what's being done, and . . . that creates enthusiasm . . . because it's ours; it's our idea."

But what does it look like to utilize an asset-based, participatory development process? There is no magic formula to achieving perfect results—development is always a process. But there are some key points that should shape our efforts:

1. How the project is done is as important as what the project is. The key is to use an empowering process that includes materially poor people as full participants in the selection, design, execution, and evaluation of the project.

2. Identify and mobilize capacities, skills, and resources of the materially poor individual or community. Celebrate their God-given potential.

3. If needed, outside resources should be used to build upon, not replace, the resources inside a community. Be careful about bringing in resources that are too much or come too early.

4. Focus on strengthening all of an individual's or a community's relationships, both formal and informal, with institutions and individuals, within the community and with outsiders.

5. Ensure that the poor people themselves are the primary actors/agents of change. Participation is NOT just a means to an end but an end in its own right.

1. List a few of your personal or your church's poverty alleviation efforts. Now look over the summary of the essentials of participatory, asset-based development in the table above. In what ways do your efforts follow or violate these principles?

2. What changes, if any, might be needed? Be specific, practical, and realistic.

DEGREES OF PARTICIPATION

(Reference *When Helping Hurts*, 139–40.)

"Asking people to be the solution to their own problem, allowing them to innovate, that's what empowerment really is." —Brad Bandy

Wanting to assist a village in Colombia with its rice production, a nonprofit organization gathered the villagers into a cooperative and bought them a thresher, a motorized huller, a generator, and a tractor. Rice production boomed, and the cooperative sold the rice at the highest price the farmers had ever received. The project appeared to be a tremendous success. The nonprofit organization then left the village, but several years later one of its staff members returned to find that the cooperative had completely disbanded and that all of the equipment was broken down and rusting away in the fields. In fact, some of the equipment had never been used at all. Yet, as the staff member walked though the village, the people pleaded with him, "If [your organization] would just come help us again, we could do so much!"[1]

1. Do you see asset-based, participatory development techniques at work in this story? How or how not?

2. How might an asset-based, participatory approach change the outcome in the above story? Why?

3. Now look over the table of different levels of participation below. Where on the continuum do you think the nonprofit in this story was functioning?

A PARTICIPATORY CONTINUUM

Mode of Participation	Type of Involvement of Local People	Relationship of Outsiders to Local People
Coercion	Local people submit to predetermined plans developed by outsiders.	doing to
Compliance	Local people are assigned to tasks, often with incentives, by outsiders; the outsiders decide the agenda and direct the process.	doing for
Consultation	Local people's opinions are asked; outsiders analyze and decide on a course of action.	doing for
Cooperation	Local people work together with outsiders to determine priorities; responsibility remains with outsiders for directing the process.	doing with
Co-Learning	Local people and outsiders share their knowledge to create appropriate goals and plans, to execute those plans, and to evaluate the results.	doing with
Community Initiated	Local people set their own agenda and mobilize to carry it out without outside initiators and facilitators.	responding to

Adapted from B. de Negri, E. Thomas, A. Ilinigumugabo, I. Muvandi, and G. Lewis, *Empowering Communities: Participatory Techniques for Community-Based Programme Development. Volume 1(2): Trainer's Manual (Participant's Handbook).* (Nairobi, Kenya: The Centre for African Family Studies. 1998), 4.

- List two ministries that you and/or your church are involved in. What level of participation by the materially poor (see the table above) do these ministries currently incorporate?

- Based on your answers above, what simple, concrete changes can you make to these programs to move them to cooperation, co-learning, or community initiated levels of participation?

UNIT 5

FOSTERING **CHANGE**

OPEN

Discuss these questions before beginning this week's unit.

• Think of a time when you took actions to effect positive change in your life. What caused you to take those actions?

• Think of an individual(s) who has had a significant, positive impact on your life. How did they do this? What did you appreciate about their approach?

Time for Change

"Thanks so much, Jerry! I don't know what I would have done without you. I am sure this will be the last time." As Tony left his office, Jerry thought, *No, it won't be the last time. You will be here* again *next month, and* again *the month after that . . . It will never end.*

Jerry put his head in his hands and thought about quitting his job . . . *again.* For the past eight years Jerry had been serving as the Mercy Coordinator for Parkview Fellowship, a thriving congregation located on one of the main thoroughfares of a mid-size, American city. For years, Parkview's senior pastor had been trying to move the congregation away from an unhealthy inward focus, urging the congregation to show the love of Christ in "Jerusalem, Judea, Samaria, and to the ends of the earth."

Jerry bought into the pastor's vision for outreach, but he was growing increasingly disillusioned. His life seemed to be an endless cycle of people like Tony, people who for a variety of reasons, *consistently* struggled to pay their electric bills, *consistently* needed help buying their groceries, and *never* seemed to change. Jerry had begun to wonder if he was just enabling people like Tony, actually hurting them in the very process of trying to help them. *We've got to change what we are doing,* he thought. *But how? Where do we begin?*

There are countless churches across North America that, like Parkview, want to engage in ministry with materially poor individuals and communities. But their efforts aren't resulting in lasting change. Something isn't working.

WATCH

Close your books and use the accompanying QR code to watch this week's video.

www.helpingwithouthurting.org/smallgroup-5

APPLY

1. Look back at your answer to the first preliminary question: what triggered you to pursue these changes?

• Had you ever attempted these changes before, but failed? If so, what was different about the attempt that finally succeeded?

2. Review the list of triggers for change below:

TRIGGERS FOR CHANGE

⚡ A recent crisis

⚡ The burden of the status quo becoming so overwhelming that people want to pursue change

⚡ The introduction of a new way of doing or seeing things that could improve people's lives

• What potential triggers for change do you see in the lives of the materially poor people around you?

• Are any of your actions fostering or undermining these triggers?

• What types of obstacles are preventing these triggers from leading to successful change? In other words, where and why does the process of change fall apart?

• Are there any ways you can better support the change process in these people's lives?

3. Given that the Holy Spirit is the one with the power to soften *all* of our hearts, in what specific ways can you pray for the people in your life who are currently unreceptive to change? In what areas of your own heart are you hardened to change?

CLOSE *(or proceed to* **Go Deeper** *if time permits)*

Remember, it is not only the materially poor who need to change. We all need to change, because we are all poor in different ways. Indeed, like many other North American churches and ministries, Parkview Fellowship is experiencing its own triggers of change, triggers that can propel it into a far more transformative and empowering approach to ministry. People like Jerry are implementing asset-based, participatory development principles in their own communities and churches. In the process, God is reworking both their hearts and the hearts of the materially poor.

PRAY

"People cannot experience lasting change without the power of the Holy Spirit. Unless God shows up and does a miracle, there cannot be lasting change."

This week, pray that God would open your eyes to see where you can invest in and support long-term, relational ministry with people who are ready to change in your community. Pray for His guidance in your work. And pray that He would soften your own heart, revealing what areas of change and healing need to occur in your life.

GO DEEPER

Use one or more of the following modules to further explore principles of poverty alleviation.

CHANGE: A PROCESS, NOT A MOMENT
(Reference *When Helping Hurts*, 207–10.)

"Remember: development is a process of ongoing change, of walking with people in a way that both they and you are brought into closer relationship with God, self, others, and the rest of creation."

Change—and thus development—doesn't happen overnight, and the end result is never guaranteed. The basic process of change can be summarized by the following diagram:

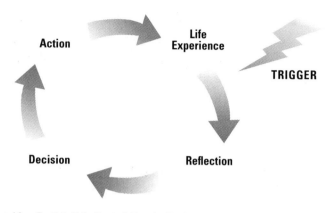

Adapted from David A. Kolb, *Experiential Learning: Experience as the Source of Learning and Development* (New Jersey: Prentice Hall, 1983).

Once a trigger for change causes some reflection, it is *not* at all automatic that the rest of the cycle will continue—major decisions, actions, or permanent changes may not occur. Indeed, a host of obstacles can get in the way of significant change. A major part of the development process is coming alongside of materially poor individuals or groups to help them remove obstacles to change that they are incapable of removing on their own, and supporting them as they remove those they can remove.

Change is a spiraling cycle of action and reflection, a learning as you go process: walk with people, trying something *together*; reflect on the experience, *together*; decide to try something additional, *together*; reflect again; try again.

Use the following questions to continue your conversation from Apply question 2, discussing examples of triggers for change in materially poor people around you.

1. Are the people you discussed in question two capable of overcoming their obstacles to change but choosing not to do so, or are they genuinely incapable of overcoming them?

2. In what intentional and practical ways are/could you and your ministry:

- Encourage people as they address the obstacles to change they *can* overcome?

- Help remove systemic obstacles to change that the poor cannot address on their own?

START WITH THE PEOPLE MOST RECEPTIVE TO CHANGE

(Reference *When Helping Hurts*, 216–21.)

"If I didn't accept their help . . . there was nothing nobody could do for me. I think that deep inside, I had to want this change . . . Yes, it was good to have someone to kind of guide you along, but you have got to want it from within." —*Freddie Weaver*

Development can only occur with people who are willing to change. If people do not believe that they are responsible to take actions to effect positive changes in their lives, it is very difficult to make progress with them. One of the most challenging elements of poverty alleviation is identifying those people who are ready to change—those who have experienced a trigger for change and are willing to embark on the process of change.

Look over the table below, and discuss the following questions:

CONTINUUM OF RECEPTIVITY TO CHANGE

Attitude of the Materially Poor Person	Approach to Moving Forward *with* Them
7. "I'm willing to demonstrate the solution to others and to advocate for change."	These responses are from people who are increasingly open and confident and who are eager for learning, information, and improved skills. It is relatively easy to move forward with them in pursuing positive change, i.e., "development." It will be relatively easy to "start soon" with them.
6. "I'm ready to try some action."	
5. "I see the problem, and I'm interested in learning more about what I could do."	
4. "I see there is a problem, but I'm afraid of changing for fear of loss."	This person has fears, often well founded, about the potential social or economic losses if they try to change. Their lives are often highly vulnerable, and they may understand the risks of potential solutions better than you do. Working with them will require listening well to their fears and concerns, modifying solutions to reduce risks, and creating a highly supportive environment.
3. "I see there is a problem, but I have my doubts that change is possible."	This person is skeptical that positive change is even possible. Their doubts may include legitimate concerns about the effectiveness of a proposed solution in their context or even the capacity of the helper. Or perhaps they have tried to change in the past and found it too difficult. Working with them requires listening well to their fears, working to build trust, and demonstrating to them that change is possible by giving examples of positive changes by others in a similar context or situation.
2. "There may be a problem, but it's not my responsibility to do anything about it."	This person believes the cause of the problem and its solution lie in the lap of the gods, or with the government, or with some outside agent. Although outside forces may be partly or even wholly responsible for their current situation, it will be extremely difficult for this person to take positive actions until they embrace their own responsibility to act in order to improve their situation.
1. "There is no problem."	This person is satisfied with things as they are, seeing no problem and no reason to change. It is impossible to make somebody change, but enabling them to persist in this condition through handouts is harmful. You need to allow them to experience the painful consequences of their decisions in hopes of triggering a desire for positive change. It may take much time and energy to help people change these attitudes, and there is no guarantee that change will occur.

INCREASING RECEPTIVITY TO POSITIVE CHANGE

DECREASING RECEPTIVITY TO POSITIVE CHANGE

Adapted from Lyra Srinivasan, *Tools for Community Participation, A Manual for Training Trainers in Participatory Techniques* (Washington, DC: PROWWESS/UNDP, 1990), 161.

1. Think of a friend or family member—whether materially poor or not—who has an area of needed change in their life. Where do they fit on this continuum, and how might you best love and support them right now?

2. In terms of poverty alleviation, would you say that you or your church and/or ministry is focused on working with people who are highly receptive to change?

3. What can you do to identify and develop relationships with people who are more receptive to change?

REMEMBER:

If you offer to walk across time with a needy individual instead of giving them handouts and they refuse your help, *you are not turning away from them; they are turning away from your help*.

LEARN THE CONTEXT AS YOU GO—GET MOVING
(Reference *When Helping Hurts*, 216.)

On the one hand, change can't begin so quickly that we do not take the time to listen well, that we fail to identify the gifts and resources of materially poor individuals or communities, or that we take charge of all aspects of the intervention. On the other hand, we must not overcorrect for this tendency by thinking we need to know everything about everybody in a community before we can get going.

Remember: Asset-based development involves *identifying, mobilizing,* and *connecting* the resources and assets within a community. A common mistake people new to asset-based development make is to try and identify *every* resource available within a community before doing anything. The point of identifying resources is to mobilize them—not just leave them catalogued in a database or listed on a spreadsheet.

• List some examples of assets of individuals, associations, and local institutions in your community that you could mobilize and connect to one another.

LOOK FOR EARLY, RECOGNIZABLE SUCCESS[1]
(Reference *When Helping Hurts*, 214–16.)

In order for people to be willing to go through the pain of change, they must have adequate enthusiasm and motivation to make initial changes and to sustain them throughout the process. Thus, as we walk alongside the materially poor, there are a few things to keep in mind:

• **Start Small**: It is hard to foster participation in big, complex changes, and such projects rarely see early success. Encourage people to set small, achievable goals, and celebrate together once these goals are met.

- **Start with What Matters—to Them:** Enter into a conversation with people about the changes that are most important to them. Sometimes these changes may not be achievable right away, may be too large, or may be dependent on other, more basic changes occurring first. But keep people's dreams and goals (so long as they are healthy and biblical) as the primary vision for change.

- **Start Soon:** Spending too much time planning and analyzing destroys people's interest in changing. Help promptly channel their enthusiasm toward meeting the goals they have set.

1. Think about the materially poor in your life. Have you asked them what types of changes and goals are most important to them?

2. Do you see any small successes they could achieve soon?

3. How might you celebrate their success together?

OUR ROLE IN THE CHANGE CYCLE—BEING A SUPPORTIVE COMMUNITY

(Reference *When Helping Hurts*, 210–13.)

"You are trying to help not only this person improve their own standing, but you are putting yourself in a situation where [you say], 'I'm humble and open enough to learn about your world as I am walking alongside of you.'" —*Jerilyn Sanders*

As a group of people who are being transformed by the gospel and who are called to be ministers of reconciliation (2 Corinthians 5:18–20), the local church *should* be the ideal community for highly relational nurturing of hurting individuals and families. But beyond meeting people's spiritual needs, the local church should also be a place that mobilizes its intangible gifts and assets on behalf of the materially poor, helping people escape the many layers of material poverty.

1. Is your church and community a place where people feel safe to admit their struggles and embark on the process of changing? What are you currently doing well, and what might you do to create an even better context for this type of vulnerability?

2. What are institutions in your community, whether an addiction support group or a prospective employer, that can help people escape poverty? How is your church linking the materially poor to these institutions?

3. Think of how you or those around you obtained their jobs. What role did their social networks play in their getting this job? What are some other ways that your social networks have helped you make positive changes in your life?

• How could you mobilize your networks on behalf of materially poor people who are interested in and ready to change?

UNIT 6

MOVING **FORWARD**

OPEN

Discuss these questions before beginning this week's unit.

- List a few of the communities in which your church or ministry is directly working, as well as a few communities in which the organizations you support are working.

- Which of the communities above are considered to be materially poor? Which of these communities are not materially poor but contain individual households that are materially poor?

What Next?

As Jerry and the rest of Parkview's leadership team explored the best way to move forward in helping people like Tony, they realized that Parkview was actually ministering in three distinct settings. First, although Parkview was not situated in a materially poor community, its visible location on a main thoroughfare made it a natural stopping point for people from all over the city or for those who were just passing through. These people could be solitary individuals, but more likely they were parts of nuclear or extended households. Second, Parkview had been providing financial support and volunteers to a ministry that was located in a materially poor neighborhood about two miles away in the same city. Finally, for many years Parkview had been sending teams to work with churches, organizations, and missionaries in materially poor communities in the Majority World.

With the framework of our previous units in mind, this unit outlines paths that a church such as Parkview and its partners can follow to pursue a more asset-based, participatory approach in their various ministry contexts.

WATCH

Close your books and use the accompanying QR code to watch this week's video.

 www.helpingwithouthurting.org/smallgroup-6

APPLY

1. Referencing the diagram below, look back at the preliminary questions to this unit. Is your church or ministry currently focused on working directly with the materially poor at the household level, or is it focused on partnering with local and international organizations working within poor communities?

THREE MINISTRY CONTEXTS

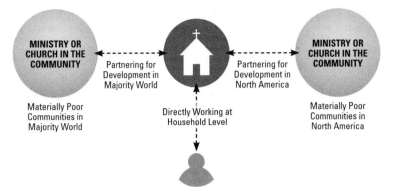

2. Have you ever been on the receiving end of the Donald Trump Effect, whether in your church, office, or family? Have you ever been pushed toward a particular action because of someone's resources, influence, or status? If so, how did it make you feel?

3. What are the implications of John 17:20–23 and Philippians 2:1–11 on the importance of linking arms with other Christians and on the attitude that we should bring to such partnerships? What are some specific actions your church or ministry could take to be an even better partner?

CLOSE *(or proceed to* **Go Deeper** *if time permits)*

If you are a North American Christian whom God has blessed with material resources, there is good news for you. As you take the first steps in helping the materially poor—namely, repenting of your own brokenness—you may discover a solution for *your* own deepest hunger: "Colossians 1 Jesus," the King who is connected to your world, the King who heals all your diseases, the King who reconciles you to God, self, others, and the rest of creation, the King who can make both you and the materially poor truly human again.

You see, in a fallen world, we are all homeless beggars. As Tim Keller explains in his book *The Prodigal God*, each one of us—whether we are materially rich or poor—is longing, like the Prodigal Son, to come home to a feast, a banquet in which all our physical needs are fully satisfied and all our relationships are completely restored, a banquet in which we experience all that it means to be human for the first time. We beggars can all come home to that wonderful feast, not through material resources or superior knowledge, but by embracing "Colossians 1 Jesus," the Master of the only banquet that can truly satisfy.[1]

PRAY

"The first step that the North American church needs to take in effective ministry to the poor at home and abroad is repentance. Repentance of pride. Repentance of a material understanding of the world. And embracing the good news of Jesus—that He can change the lives of poor people, including me."

As you move forward in helping without hurting, rejoice that you serve a God who is making all things new, restoring all things to the way He originally intended them to be. Celebrate the reality that His victory over sin and death is certain, thanks to Christ's sacrifice. And pray for His wisdom and guidance as you humbly proclaim that good news to others in both word and deed.

GO DEEPER

Use one or more of the following modules to further explore principles of poverty alleviation.

HEALTHY PARTNERSHIPS: AVOIDING THE DONALD TRUMP EFFECT
(Reference *When Helping Hurts*, 239–41.)

Partnering for Development in the Majority World

MINISTRY OR
CHURCH IN THE
COMMUNITY

Partnering for
Development in
Majority World

Materially Poor
Communities in
Majority World

"I think almost anywhere you are . . . some group is doing decent work. Start supporting them . . . and be willing to do what they need, versus what you want to do."

When a middle- to upper-class North American walks into a poor community—particularly in the Majority World—they are often seen as Donald Trump, a rich, powerful, and influential person. As a result, everything we say carries more weight than we intend, creating the expectation that we will be their saviors and that our ideas must be implemented. There are several guidelines, though, that can help us avoid accidentally being Donald Trump in our partnerships.

• Work hard to develop truthful and transparent relationships with your partners over time. Sticking with them, even when they fail, builds trust.

• Be less visible. Support trainers and churches within the local community so that "Donald Trump" is not seen or heard.

• Be extremely hesitant to make "suggestions."

• Be sure that local people are contributing their own time, money, or other resources to the project.

1. If your church partners with other churches or organizations that minister to materially poor people, whether at home or abroad, do those other churches or organizations appreciate the help your church provides them? How do you know?

2. Have you ever seen the Donald Trump Effect at work in your own ministry efforts? Do you or your church need to repent of any ways it has acted toward its partners?

BEING A DIFFERENT TYPE OF PARTNER

(Reference *When Helping Hurts,* 229–43.)

"Your role is to support the churches and ministries that God has already placed there, enabling them through your prayers, encouragement, and financial support to engage in a highly relational, asset-based participatory process."

Development ministries desperately need financial supporters who understand what poverty alleviation is really about—reconciling the four key relationships—and who are willing to fund the long and winding process that must be used to get there.

But in addition to being a good financial partner, there are other ways North American individuals and churches can be good partners:

• Praying

• Providing words of encouragement

• Helping to conduct asset-mapping exercises

• Supplying mentoring teams for low-income households

• Providing jobs and/or job referrals to residents of the community

• Linking community members to potential networks

• Serving on the board of a local organization

• Providing counsel (only when asked)

1. Out of the above actions, are there any areas where you think you could be even more supportive of your ministry partners?

2. In what ways can you hold each other accountable to follow through on the actions you listed above?

DIRECTLY WORKING AT THE HOUSEHOLD LEVEL

(Use in conjunction with *When Helping Hurts*, 224–29.)

When your church is considering how to directly minister to the materially poor, your work must be based on the asset-based, participatory approach to poverty alleviation we discussed in Units Four and Five. The following steps provide a brief outline of how your church can begin this process. The steps are further explained and unpacked in the Getting Started section at the end of this unit.

Directly Working at
Household Level

• **Step One**: Assess and mobilize the gifts of your church or ministry.

• **Step Two**: Learn about the existing ministries and organizations in the area where you want to work, including both private and government-based entities. Find out how your church can engage with these institutions.

• **Step Three**: Adopt asset-based, participatory, "first encounter" policies to help guide your congregation or group when materially poor people approach it for help.

• **Step Four**: Explore the possibility of starting a new ministry to address key gaps that aren't being addressed by existing ministries or organizations.

1. What do you currently do when someone walks into your church asking for material assistance? Does your response reflect an asset-based, participatory understanding of material poverty alleviation? What might you further improve?

2. Commit to working through the Getting Started section, which will help you apply the principles of this series in your own context when working at the household level. Spend time reading over it together, sharing your initial thoughts. Dedicate time to working through these questions in the following weeks.

GETTING STARTED

IMPLEMENTING AN ASSET-BASED, PARTICIPATORY DEVELOPMENT APPROACH

(Use in conjunction with chapters 10 and 11 of *When Helping Hurts*.)

Review the following four steps, discussing and noting who, how, what, and when your church might start designing and implementing each step in your particular context. Further, discuss where each of you personally can contribute to the process. (See Suggested Resources to use in this process.)

- **Step One**: Assess and mobilize the gifts of your church or ministry. Find out through questionnaires, interviews, or other information-gathering strategies what your church or group has to offer.

- Assess individual assets within your own church: Who has the maturity, relational skills, networks, passion, and willingness to invest time in a long-term relationship with the materially poor? Who has administrative and organizational skills to help lead a development ministry?

- Identify and mobilize these people, training them in the principles of poverty alleviation.

- **Step Two**: Learn about the existing ministries and organizations in the area where you want to work.

- Discover and appreciate what is already happening in your community and in these organizations, ensuring that you don't needlessly "reinvent the wheel" or undermine an existing ministry.

- Establish relationships with any existing ministries, and develop concrete processes to help connect the materially poor to these organizations.

- **Step Three**: Adopt asset-based, participatory, "first encounter" policies to help guide your congregation or group when materially poor people approach it for help.

  - Does your church or ministry have benevolence policies in place already?

    If so, are they consistent with an asset-based, participatory, development approach? If not, what are the steps you could take to move in that direction?

  - Craft a tactful, gracious series of questions to determine whether someone asking your church for assistance (1) needs relief, rehabilitation, or development and (2) is receptive to change. (See Suggested Resources for examples.)

  - Direct those who are willing to change toward the equipped members of your congregation and/or other community organizations that can partner with them in the change process.

- **Step Four**: Explore the possibility of starting a new ministry. Has your work in steps one through three revealed a need for development work that you are capable of offering?

  - As you start your ministry, who are key members from within the materially poor community whom you can involve in the change process?

  - Research similar ministries working in other cities and communities. What ministry models from these areas might you reference as you begin your work?

SUGGESTED RESOURCES

- *Ministry Inventory Guide: Assess Your Church's Ministry Capacity and Identity* Provides useful information for asset-mapping within your church or organization (http://communities firstassociation.org/ministry-inventory-guide/)

- *United Way 2-1-1 Resource Guide* Provides information on existing organizations and ministries in your area (www.referweb. net/211CommunityResources/)

- *Guidelines for Benevolence*—**Diaconal Ministries Canada** Provides first response questions and policies (http://www.diaconal ministries.com/resources/docs/guidelinesForBenevolence.pdf)

- *Communities First Association* Offers community organizing and development resources (http://communitiesfirstassociation.org)

- *The Beauty of Partnership Study Guide* Provides a helpful summary of key principles in being a good partner with ministries and churches (http://beautyofpartnership.org/)

- *The Lausanne Standards: Affirmations and Agreements for Giving and Receiving Money in Mission* Provides carefully developed guidelines for how to financially partner with ministries and churches without causing unintentional harm (www.lausanne standards.org)

NOTES

Unit 1: Reconsidering the Meaning of Poverty

1. This section draws on Bryant L. Myers, *Walking with the Poor: Principles and Practices of Transformational Development* (Maryknoll, N.Y.: Orbis Books, 1999).

2. Ibid., 86.

3. This section draws on Darrow L. Miller with Stan Guthrie, *Discipling the Nations: The Power of Truth to Transform Cultures* (Seattle, WA: YWAM, 2001), 31–46.

Unit 2: Seeing God at Work

1. Alisa Collins's story can be viewed in Tod Lending, *Legacy*, DVD (Chicago: Nomadic Pictures, 1999).

Unit 3: Understanding Why Good Intentions Are Not Enough

1. This is a modification of the definition of paternalism found in Roland Bunch, *Two Ears of Corn: A Guide to People-Centered Agricultural Improvement* (Oklahoma City: World Neighbors, 1982).

2. Alvin Mbola, "Bad Relief Undermines Worship in Kibera," *Mandate*, Chalmers Center for Economic Development, 2007, no. 3, available at www.chalmers.org.

3. Bryant L. Myers, *Walking with the Poor: Principles and Practices of Transformational Development* (Maryknoll, N.Y.: Orbis Books, 1999), 65–66.

Unit 4: Joining God's Work

1. Roland Bunch, *Two Ears of Corn: A Guide to People-Centered Agricultural Improvement* (Oklahoma City: World Neighbors, 1982), 18–19.

Unit 5: Fostering Change

1. This section draws heavily on Roland Bunch, *Two Ears of Corn: A Guide to People-Centered Agricultural Improvement* (Oklahoma City: World Neighbors, 1982), 21–36.

Unit 6: Moving Forward

1. Timothy Keller, *The Prodigal God: Recovering the Heart of the Christian Faith* (New York: Dutton, 2008), 107, 132–33.

ACKNOWLEDGMENTS

This project would not have been possible without the encouragement and work of countless people, including:

Katie Casselberry of the Chalmers Center, who structured, shaped, and shepherded this project from beginning to end. If anything in this book makes sense, it is because of her!

Cathi Linch, Jeff Galley, Jonathan Meisner, Brian Lawes, and all the other folks at LifeChurch.tv who have championed the message of When Helping Hurts and have created the videos that accompany this project. Your generosity and partnership continue to be an enormous blessing both to our work and to us personally.

Our team at Moody Publishers who faithfully worked to make this project a reality, particularly Duane Sherman, Barnabas Piper, and Pam Pugh. It is a privilege to work with people who share our vision for seeing the church serve as ambassadors of reconciliation around the world.

The staff of the Chalmers Center, especially Andy Jones and Randy Russ, who helped this project reach the light of day.

The countless people who agreed to share their stories and expertise in the video series, including Patrice Azebbar, Brad Bandy, Sarah Kasule, Robert Lupton, Alvin Mbola, Michael Matheson Miller, Katie Nienow, Rachel Sang, Freddie Weaver, Joel Soti, and many others. Thank you for taking the time to share your unique perspectives.

The mission leaders and pastors at churches around the country who have encouraged the Chalmers Center along the way and are advancing Christ's kingdom in exciting ways: Curtis Alan, Joel Assaraff, Pradip Ayer, Steve Baker, Ron Barnes, Jonathan Bean, Laurie Beshore,

Geoff Bradford, Ryan Britt, Dan Burns, Ron Burdock, Josh Butler, Jo Anne Clark, Mike Constantz, Jim Davis, Alicia Divers, Jeremy Fair, Eddie Foster, JD Greear, Gus Gustafson, Josie Guth, Jonathan Henry, Tracy Hipps. Glenn Hoburg, Mark Hoffschneider, Jerry Ireland, Shawn Janes, David Juelfs, Ananda Kumar, Oscar Leiva, Justin Lopez, Rod MacIlvaine, Jay Madden, Victor Martinez, Brent McKinney, Rod Miles, Eli Morris, Billy Nolan, David O'Dowd, Mike Oakes, Matt Olthoff, Elli Oswald, Kevin Palau, Mark Perraut, Brian Petak, Tod Rasmuson, Chris Rich, Jim Romack, Matt Seadore, Suzie Steen, Jeff Story, Adam Tarnow, Ben Taylor, Jonathan Todd, Judy Van Dyke, Bryson Volgetanz, Jeff Ward, Martin Wegner, Judi Wheeler, Ben Wikner, Jason Williams, Myron Williams, Andy Wineman, and countless others.

But above all, we would like to praise God for His ongoing goodness and patience. Without His reconciling work in our lives, none of this would be possible. May His name continue to be glorified as the church proclaims the good news that Jesus Christ is making all things new.

—Steve Corbett and Brian Fikkert

CHECK OUT
WHEN HELPING HURTS!

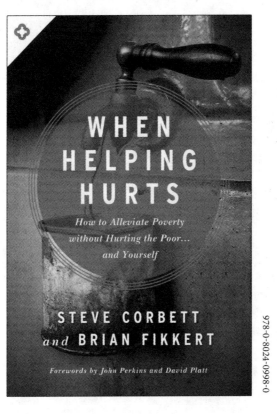

978-0-8024-0998-0

Also available as an ebook

MOODY
PUBLISHERS

Move your church forward in helping without hurting.

The Chalmers Center equips churches and ministries with gospel-driven tools designed to point the materially poor to Jesus and produce sustained transformation. Whether you are working with the poor in North America or the Majority World, the Chalmers Center has opportunities for you to be equipped for positive change.

Maria, a single mother, walks into your church's office asking for help paying her electric bill.

What do you do?

The Chalmers Center's *Faith & Finances* program

equips churches to empower people like Maria, fostering long-term transformation rather than merely providing temporary handouts. Through *Faith & Finances* classes, your church can train Maria in practical money management skills. In the process, both you and Maria can explore who God is, what gifts He has given you, and how your money is a part of His work in the world.

The Chalmers Center

Get your church trained, visit
www.chalmers.org/finances

MOODYRADIO

Where you turn. For life.

Moody Radio produces and delivers compelling programs filled with biblical insights and creative expressions of faith that help you take the next step in your relationship with Christ.

You can hear Moody Radio on 34 stations and more than 1,500 radio outlets across the U.S. and Canada. Or listen on your smartphone with the Moody Radio app!

www.moodyradio.org